T0271767

THE
DECEMBER
BABY

By Noel Streatfeild and available from Headline

The January Baby

The February Baby

The March Baby

The April Baby

The May Baby

The June Baby

The July Baby

The August Baby

The September Baby

The October Baby

The November Baby

The December Baby

THE
December
BABY

★

Noel Streatfeild

Copyright © Noel Streatfeild 1959
Copyright © The beneficiaries of the estate of Noel Streatfeild 1986
Excluding the illustrations on pages iii, v, 6, 24, 25, 28, 29, 30, 65, 69, 76, 82
© Becky Cameron 2023

The right of Noel Streatfeild to be identified as the Author of the Work has been
asserted by her in accordance with the Copyright, Designs and Patents Act 1988.

First published in 1959
This edition published in 2023 by Headline Home
an imprint of Headline Publishing Group

1

Apart from any use permitted under UK copyright law, this publication may
only be reproduced, stored, or transmitted, in any form, or by any means, with prior
permission in writing of the publishers or, in the case of reprographic production,
in accordance with the terms of licences issued by the Copyright Licensing Agency.

Every effort has been made to fulfil requirements with regard to reproducing copyright material.
The author and publisher will be glad to rectify any omissions at the earliest opportunity.

Cataloguing in Publication Data is available from the British Library

Hardback ISBN 978 1 0354 0861 0
eISBN 978 1 0354 0862 7

Typeset in 14.75/15pt Centaur MT Pro by Jouve (UK), Milton Keynes

Printed and bound in Great Britain by Clays Ltd, Elcograf S.p.A.

Headline's policy is to use papers that are natural, renewable and recyclable
products and made from wood grown in well-managed forests and other
controlled sources. The logging and manufacturing processes are expected
to conform to the environmental regulations of the country of origin.

HEADLINE PUBLISHING GROUP
An Hachette UK Company
Carmelite House
50 Victoria Embankment
London EC4Y 0DZ

www.headline.co.uk
www.hachette.co.uk

CONTENTS

This book contains examples of historical cures and home remedies. These are included for historical interest only and should not be followed. If your child is unwell, consult a doctor or other medical professional. Neither the author nor the publisher accept any liability for any loss or damage caused by the application of any of the information or suggestions in this book.

YOUR December baby has arrived. The good news has been passed round your family and friends. Now the day has come when you are allowed visitors, and the question is being asked, 'What present shall I bring?'

It was Robert Louis Stevenson who had the perfect idea for a present for a December baby. He knew that the nearer you are born to Christmas, the less a child's chances of having a real birthday, and how right he was; being a Christmas Eve baby myself, I know. So to a small girl born at Christmas-time he made a gift of his own birthday – not a very nice one, for he was born in November – but still a better birthday than her own which he took in exchange. So if you have a friend who is willing, and has a birthday in a pleasant month, ask for their birthday for your December baby; an August birthday would be an ideal present.

Christmas preparations or aftermath apart,

December is an awkward month for presents.
Flowers are scarce, and terribly expensive. The
lucky ones who have gardens can bring dear
little bunches which may contain almost
anything, from winter jasmine, which is
seasonal, to a rosebud which does not know it
is December. There are of course Christmas
roses, and early forced spring flowers, and
cyclamen in pots for those who can afford
them, but for those whose purses are lean,

3

something other than flowers will have to be chosen.

It is very hard in December to resist bringing your baby a toy. All the year round that department called 'soft toys' is difficult to resist, but at Christmas impossible. Lion cubs jostle blue-eyed lambs, pink monkeys hold out pleading arms, and poodles made apparently of real wool gaze down at you soulfully from a shelf. But do you really want a lion cub, pink monkey, blue-eyed lamb, or a woolly poodle, and your baby certainly will

4

not. The present may seem charming while lying on your bed, but it will be a shocking dust collector while it is waiting for baby to

be old enough to enjoy it. So if heads are kept, toys are out.

Something for you or the baby to wear makes a wonderful present, but the chances are that no friend or relative has been able to hold up presenting the baby clothes they have made, or bought, until your baby actually arrived, for the temptation to post the parcel at once, while both blue and pink are correct,

is overwhelming. As for you, you will be lucky if you get anything very luxurious so near to Christmas: hearts will be willing, but purses will be weak.

Years of saying 'What shall I bring her?' has resulted in these books, one for each month. Each opens with lists of names suitable for the month. It is odd, but many parents in spite of months of talking it over, can still be arguing about names on the way to the christening. The first name may be chosen, but it sounds wrong somehow with the surname, so another is needed. Or the parents may have been so certain that it was to be a boy, or vice versa, that when the wrong sex turned up no names were ready. It is for such parents the name pages were compiled.

Few of us can resist glancing at what the stars foretell, even if we don't believe a word that is written. So here for believers and unbelievers alike is what is prophesied for Sagittarius and Capricorn babies. This, either to back up your beliefs or disbeliefs, is followed by a list of some of the distinguished people born on each day in the month, and very surprising reading much of it is. I studied my own birth date and find myself sharing the day with Elizabeth, Empress of Austria, Ava Gardner, King John, Saint Ignatius of Loyola and Matthew Arnold: a varied group, but did they or do they, and incidentally myself, share the qualities Capricorn babies are supposed to possess? Now have a look at your baby's birth date.

NAMES
for the
DECEMBER
BABY

THE Saxons, after they had been converted to Christianity, called December Holy-month. *Helga, Olga,* and *Sanchia* mean 'holy', *Heloise* and *Heloisa* 'famous holiness', *Christian* 'follower of Christ', and the girl's versions of *Christian* are *Christiana, Christina, Christine* and *Kirstin*. *Christabel* and *Christabelle* mean 'the handsome anointed one'. *Dominic* and *Dominica* mean 'of the Lord'. *Jerome* means 'sacred name', and *Christopher* 'Christ-bearing'.

Because he is a popular nursery favourite, it is almost impossible to think of *Christopher* and not add *Robin*, and as well *Robin* is a Christmassy bird; the name means 'bright fame'. *Elinor* means 'bright one', and so do *Elaine, Eleanor, Eleanora, Ellen, Helen, Lena, Lenora, Lenore* and *Leonore*.

9

The apostle assigned to December is St Paul. *Paul* means 'little'.

The 6th of December is St Nicolas' Day, the fourth century saint, who in England is called 'Father Christmas'. The red outfit he wears comes from Russia, where St Nicolas is the patron saint. The name *Nicolas* means 'victory of the people'. It has the alternative form *Nicol*. For girls it becomes *Nicola*, *Nicolette* and *Colette*.

The 13th of December is St Lucy's Day. *Lucy* means 'the light' and has the additional forms

Lucia, *Lucilla*, *Lucilia* and *Lucinda*. For boys *Lucian* and *Lucius* mean 'light' too.

December the 25th, being Christmas Day, brings many names to mind. First of course *Mary*, which means 'wished-for child'. It has all these variations: *Marita*, *Marian*, *Marianne*, *Marie*,

Mariel, Marion, Marlene, Marylyn, Maura, Maureen, Maurine and *Miriam*. Then *Joseph* which means 'may Jehovah increase'. Although correctly they belong to the feast of the Epiphany, most people think of the Wise Men on Christmas Day. *Melchior* means 'king of light'; and other kingly names are *Rex*, which simply means 'king', and *Tiernan*, 'kingly'.

The 26th of December is St Stephen's Day, the day when 'Good King Wenceslas looked

out'. *Stephen* means 'crown'; the girl's version is *Stephanie*.

The 31st is St Sylvester's Day. *Sylvester* or

Silvester mean 'of the forest'. Other names with similar meanings are *Silas, Silvan* and *Sylvan*, which mean 'forest'. *Talbot* means 'to cut a faggot', and there are some shrub names: *Ivo* 'yew', *Lawrence* or *Laurence* 'laurel', and for a girl *Daphne* which means 'bay-tree'.

Apart from the religious association, there are of course many Christmas names. *Noel, Nowell,* or *Noelle, Yule* for a boy, *Carol* for either a boy or girl, or how about *Holly*? From *Holly* there are three names which mean 'red': *Rory, Roy* and *Russell.*

A December baby is often called a Christmas present. *Dolly, Dorothea, Dorothy, Theodora, Theodore, Tudor, Matthew* and *Nathaniel* all mean 'gift of God'. *Dora, Doris* and *Dorinda* all mean 'gift', and so does *Nathan. Isadore* or *Isadora* for a girl, mean 'gift of Isis'.

December is the month of children's plays. *Peter Pan* comes first to mind. *Peter* means 'stone'. *Wendy* means 'wanderer'. Then there is *Alice in Wonderland. Alice* means 'truth', as do *Alicia, Alison* and *Alys.* There may be a film or television serial of *Little*

Lord Fauntleroy — *Cedric* means 'war-chief' — or perhaps scenes acted from *Uncle Tom's Cabin*. *Eva* means 'lively', as do *Eve* and *Eveleen*. Because of *A Christmas Carol*, Dickens is accounted a Christmas writer. There are many names from his books. Tiny Tim is

the very spirit of Christmas. *Timothy* means 'honour God'. Pip's full name is Philip Pirip. *Philip* means 'horse-lover', and becomes for a girl *Philippa*. *Oliver* in *Oliver Twist* comes from 'the olive tree'. For girls *Olive* and *Olivia* mean 'olive'. From *David Copperfield*, *David* means 'friend', and friend provides a string of names: *Alwyn* (*Aylwin*) 'noble friend', *Edwin* 'rich friend', or *Edwina* for a girl, *Mervin* (*Mervyn*) 'famous friend', and *Harding* 'firm friend'.

Then there are the pantomimes. Cinderella's real name was presumably *Ella*, which means 'all'. The Giant Killer is *Jack*. *Jack* is one of many forms of *John*, 'The Lord's Grace'. Other names with the same meaning are *Evan, Hans, Iain* or *Ian, Ivan, Jan, Jon, Sean, Shawn* and *Shane*. Hansel and Grethel are really John and Margaret. *Margaret*, which means 'pearl', has not only the form *Greta*, but all these others too: *Maisie, Margery, Margot, Marguerite, Marjorie, Marjory* and *Rita*.

Finally flower names. A Christmas rose is

inseparable from Christmas, so how about *Rose*? Or there is the winter Jasmine; *Jasmine* is a lovely name. For the fortunate who can persuade them to grow, there is the exquisite iris stylosa, and *Iris* is a charming name.

Last of all as a December suggestion, how about *Angel*, most appropriate, and though your son may grow up to scold you for choosing it, a name more suited to a boy than to a girl.

GIFTS
for the
DECEMBER
BABY

IF a godparent or other well-wisher would like to give the baby a piece of jewellery, the right stone for December is the turquoise, which is the emblem of prosperity. Mothers of December babies will approve their offspring's choice of birthstone, for the turquoise is an inexpensive yet pretty stone, and it is likely amongst the christening presents the December baby will be given a gold brooch or pin set with turquoises. Here is what Leonardus has written in 1750 about this stone in *The Mirror of Stones*:

'There is a vulgar Opinion, that it is useful to Horsemen, and that so long as the Rider has it with him, his Horse will never tire him, and will preserve him unhurt from any Accident. It strengthens the Sight with its Aspect. It is said to defend him that carries it from outward and evil Casualties.'

The charming old custom of arranging flowers or berries in a vase or bunch, so that it brings a message, is almost forgotten today. But if your December baby should receive a Christmassy garland of holly and mistletoe, the message will be: By foresight (holly) you will surmount your difficulties (mistletoe).

If your baby was born between the 1st and the 21st of December read pages 24 and 25, but if between the 22nd and the 31st skip to pages 26 and 27.

UNDER
WHAT STARS WAS
MY BABY
BORN?

SAGITTARIUS
The Archer

23rd November–21st December

CAPRICORN
The Sea Goat

22nd December–20th January

AQUARIUS
The Water Bearer

21st January–19th February

PISCES
The Fishes

20th February–20th March

ARIES
The Ram

21st March–20th April

TAURUS
The Bull

21st April–21st May

GEMINI
The Twins

22nd May–21st June

CANCER
The Crab

22nd June–23rd July

LEO
The Lion

24th July–23rd August

VIRGO
The Virgin

24th August–23rd September

LIBRA
The Scales

24th September–23rd October

SCORPIO
The Scorpion

24th October–22nd November

Sagittarius — the Archer
23rd November—21st December

PEOPLE born under Sagittarius are active, both physically and mentally. They are most at home out of doors, have a preference for work in the open air and are keen on sports. They are kind-hearted, sympathetic and impulsive, somewhat indiscriminate in their choice of friends. They do demand sincerity in others though, and are quick to note the lack of it. This acute power of insight is indeed so developed in some Sagittarius people as to amount almost to a gift of prophecy. Physically Sagittarians are well-formed. Their facial expression is open and pleasing, their eyes always remarkable. They talk freely and love light-heartedly.

For the Sagittarius Baby

Lucky to wear chrysolite, uncut and deep amethyst, carbuncle.
Lucky stones are granite, sandstone.
Lucky metal is tin.
The Sagittarius baby's colour is violet.
Lucky number is 3.
Luckiest day is Thursday.

Capricorn — the Sea Goat
22nd December–20th January

PEOPLE born under Capricorn are deep thinkers, ambitious for intellectual attainments and political power. They are good organisers and often splendid orators, speaking rapidly and urgently. They are self-reliant and proud, yet very persistent and patient. Their magnetism and self-possession make them good teachers. Capricorn people are faithful and sincere in their affections, but they are not demonstrative. Their crust of apparent selfishness covers little vanity, but a real earnestness. They are more capable of carrying out large undertakings than people of any other sign.

For the Capricorn Baby

Lucky to wear a sapphire.
Lucky stones are jet, onyx and lapis lazuli.
Lucky metal is lead.
The Capricorn baby's colour is indigo.
Lucky number is 8.
Luckiest day is Saturday.

BABIES BORN
ON
THE SAME DAY
AS
YOUR BABY

IS there any special good fortune in being born on one particular day? Is there any truth in a horoscope – will babies born under Sagittarius grow up like this, and those born under the sign of Capricorn grow up to be like that? Here is a list to help make up your mind whether there is any truth in what the stars foretell.

1st   Queen Alexandra, 1844. Helen Simpson, 1897. Keith Michell, 1926.

2nd   Georges Seurat, 1859. Dame Irene Vanbrugh, 1872. Sir John Barbirolli, 1899.

3rd   Ludvig Holberg, 1684. Frederick Lord Leighton, 1830. Dr Rajendra Prasad, 1884. Nigel Balchin, 1908.

4th   Madame Récamier, 1777. Thomas Carlyle, 1795. Edith Cavell, 1856. Rainer Maria Rilke, 1875.

5th   Robert Harley, 1st Earl of Orford, 1661. Christina Rossetti, 1830. Admiral Lord

Jellicoe, 1859. Walt Disney, 1901. Werner Heisenberg, 1901. Lord Packenham, 1905.

6th Henry VI, 1421. General George Monck, 1608. Warren Hastings, 1732. Mrs Masham, 1734. Joseph Conrad, 1857. Sir Osbert Sitwell, 1892. Eve Curie, 1904.

7th Saint Columba, 521. Mary, Queen of Scots, 1542. Henry Stuart, Lord Darnley, 1545. Joyce Cary, 1888.

8th Queen Christina of Sweden, 1626. Bjørnstjerne Bjørnson, 1832. Jan Sibelius, 1865. Diego Rivera, 1886. James Thurber, 1894.

9th Gustavus Adolphus the Great of Sweden, 1594. John Milton, 1608. Francis Rawdon-Hastings, 1st Marquis of Hastings, 1754. Joel Chandler Harris (Uncle Remus), 1848. Hermione Gingold, 1897. R. A. Butler, 1902. Douglas Fairbanks Jr, 1909.

10th Thomas Holcroft, 1745. Eugène Sue, 1804. César Franck, 1822. Emily Dickinson, 1830. Frances Evelyn Maynard, Countess of Warwick, 1861. Ernest H. Shepard, 1879. Field Marshal the Earl Alexander of Tunis, 1891.

11th   Pope Leo X, 1475. Hector Berlioz, 1803. Alfred de Musset, 1810. Robert Koch, 1843. Robert Henriques, 1905.

12th   Anne of Denmark, queen of James I, 1574. Admiral Lord Hood, 1724. William Henry, 1774. Marie Louise, Empress of the French, 1791. Gustave Flaubert, 1821. Edward G. Robinson, 1893

13th   Duc de Sully, 1560. Heinrich Heine, 1797. Princess Marina, Duchess of Kent, 1906. Van Heflin, 1908.

14th   Nostradamus, 1503. Tycho Brahe, 1546. Admiral Lord Cochrane, 1775. George VI, 1895. Paul I of Greece, 1901.

15th   Nero, A.D. 37. Katharine of Aragon, 1485. La Rochefoucauld, 1613. Jerome Bonaparte, (King of Westphalia), 1784. Sir Alfred East, 1849. General Sir Miles C. Dempsey, 1896.

16th   Jane Austen, 1775. Beethoven, 1770. Mary Russell Mitford, 1787. Sir Jack Hobbs, 1882. Noel Coward, 1899.

17th   Prince Rupert, 1619. Emilie de Breteuil, Marquise du Châtelet, 1706. Sir Humphrey Davy, 1778. John Greenleaf

Whittier, 1809. MacKenzie King, 1874. Jacobus Strauss, Q.C., 1900.

18th   Elizabeth Petrovna, Empress of Russia, 1709. Joseph Stalin, 1879. Rebecca West, 1892. Sir Joseph Thomson, 1856. H. H. Munroe ('Saki'), 1870. Paul Klee, 1879. Gladys Cooper, 1889. Christopher Fry, 1907. Celia Johnson, 1908. Prince William of Gloucester, 1941.

19th   Philip V of Spain, 1683. Sir William Edward Parry, 1790. Lord Rowallan, 1895. Sir Ralph Richardson, 1902. Edith Piaf, 1915.

20th   Richard Oastler, 1789. Thomas Graham, 1805. Ethel Sidgwick, 1877. Robert Gordon Menzies, 1894.

21st   Jean Racine, 1639. Benjamin Disraeli, Earl of Beaconsfield, 1804. Rebecca West, 1892. Sir Harold Anthony Caccia, 1905.

22nd   Sara Coleridge, 1802. Lucien Petipa, 1815. Dame Peggy Ashcroft, 1907.

23rd   Sir Richard Arkwright, 1732. Charles Augustin Sainte-Beuve, 1804. Lord Rank, 1888. Marshal of the R.A.F. Lord Douglas, 1893. Crown Prince Akihito of Japan, 1933.

24th King John, 1167. Saint Ignatius of Loyola, 1491. Matthew Arnold, 1822. Elizabeth, Empress of Austria, 1837. Ava Gardner, 1922.

25th Jan De Witt, 1625. Sir Isaac Newton, 1642. Dorothy Wordsworth, 1771. Mohammed Ali Jinnah, 1876. Humphrey Bogart, 1899. Duchess of Gloucester, 1901. Princess Alexandra, 1936.

26th Thomas Gray, 1716. Romney, 1734. Mary Somerville, 1780. Sir Norman Angell, 1874. Derick Heathcoat-Amory, 1899. Richard Widmark, 1914.

27th Johann Kepler, 1571. Pope Pius VI, 1717. Louis Pasteur, 1822. Nicholas Legat, 1869. Marlene Dietrich, 1901.

28th Woodrow Wilson, 1856. St John Ervine, 1883.

29th Marquise de Pompadour, 1721. Charles Macintosh, 1766. William Ewart Gladstone, 1809. Elizabeth, queen of Carol I of Romania, 1843. Pablo Casals, 1876.

30th Titus, Roman Emperor, 41 A.D. Rudyard Kipling, 1865. Stephen Leacock, 1869.

L. P. Hartley, 1895. Sir Carol Reed, 1906.

31st   Andreas Vesalius, 1514. Prince Charles Edward Stuart, 1720. General Charles Cornwallis, 1st Marquess, 1738. Henri Matisse, 1869. Peter May, 1929.

36

THE
UPBRINGING
OF DECEMBER
BABIES
OF
THE
PAST

PLEASING AMUSEMENT with excellent Exercise. – G. GROSVENOR most respectfully begs leave to acquaint the Nobility and Gentry, that he is happy in having it in his power to remove the great inconvenience so long complained of in sending KITES to distant parts, on account of the extreme aukwardness and expence of the package, having brought to perfection curious Kites, on a new construction, rendered so portable that they may be sent to any part of the world with the greatest ease imaginable. Sold only at Grosvenor's Perfumery Warehouse and Toy Rooms, No. 303, Holborn. The greatest variety of Rocking Horses, of various sizes and colours, with Toys of every description, sold extremely cheap, by trading entirely for ready money.

The Times, 1798.

A Bath for the Rickets, Livergrown, or Obstructions of the Liver in a Child – Take a Sheepshead with the Wool on it, clave it in the middle, and boil it till it be tender, that the bones slip clean out of the flesh, boiling with it Smallage, Camomil, Primrose leaves and Hysop of each four handfuls; then bathe the Child all over with this Broth, as hot as can be endur'd twice a day; then mash the Herbs with the Flesh, and bind it on warm to the joints that are weak.

Hartman, *The Family Physitian*, 1696.

We have every reason to believe that catarrhal affections have been produced by the use of cold water, especially to very young children, from which the poor little creatures have escaped with much difficulty. Now, as serious evils may arise from ablutions of cold water, and as we have never heard it even suggested that immediate injury has followed the use of warm, the line of conduct to be pursued would seem to be very easy to make choice of.

Some, with a view to improve the quality of the water, add brandy or other liquors to it; or if they do not mingle these with the water, they very carefully wash the infant's head with some one of them, for the purpose, they say, of strengthening it. This practice, though not so extensively injurious as the one just spoken of, is nevertheless decidedly improper. There cannot be any possible necessity for thus violently stimulating the poor babe – thus do they 'banish simplicity from even dressing a new born child'.

A Treatise on the Physical and Medical Treatment of Children,
by William P. Dewees, 1826.

When baby is, as we say familiarly, 'shortened', it is a good plan to adopt cotton socks under the woollen ones; they are very comfortable to the child, and it is as well to delay the putting on of the smart little red and blue shoes, with which it is our pride to adorn our baby's feet, as long as he is in nurse's arms; the woollen socks are so easily washed, and the cotton fabric of the under sock gives excellent protection to the feet.

Many persons object to high dresses for a babe, on the very reasonable ground that the size of its garments must increase every day, and that they cannot be made to fit with any degree of nicety without runners round the neck of the bodice; these runners in high dresses just get into the creases of the child's neck, and consequently chafe it. This, however, may be easily remedied by the use of an old cambric handkerchief, placed shawl-wise, crossed over the breast and stitched behind. It does not disfigure the dress, and takes all the pressure of the runners from the neck.

In the place of that cumbrous cloak and cape, for an outdoor garment, we would venture to suggest a skirt and jacket, the sleeves of the latter leaving the child's arms free. We know a lady who has adopted this dress with great comfort to the child and nurse; the nurse can clasp the baby safely in her arms, without the obstruction of a heavy cape interfering with her movements.

Infant Life, by E. N. G., 1869.

A child, a year and a half old, had a very bad scarlet fever . . . In all such cases, wine is the only anchor of hope. Port wine was procured, and lest it might be too strong, the spirit was partly burned out of it, though we think it would have been better to mix it with water. A teaspoonful was given at short intervals, till it was evident that the spirit began to affect the little patient, whose eyes became brighter and his mouth more moist and comfortable. After a few hours he fell asleep, and awakened in a fair state of recovery.

Buchan, *The Cottage Physician*, 1825.

Rome. 26th December 1863. Today after lunch we went to St Stefano Rotondo, thence to the

Ara Cœli to hear the little children preach, which was very funny. Quaint little souls of five and six, put up on the side of a pillar, hold forth with abundant action about the Nativity, as if they had seen it.

Life, Journal and Letters of Henry Alford, D.D., 1873.

While I lay musing on my pillow, I heard a sound of little feet pattering outside of the door, and a whispered consultation. Presently a choir of small voices chanted forth an old Christmas carol, the burden of which was: —

Rejoice, our Saviour he was born
On Christmas-day in the morning.

I rose softly, slipped on my clothes, opened the door suddenly, and beheld one of the most beautiful little fairy groups that a painter could imagine. It consisted of a boy and two girls, the eldest not more than six, and lovely as seraphs. They were going the round of the house, and singing at every chamber-door; but my sudden appearance frightened them into mute bashfulness. They remained for a moment playing upon their lips with their fingers, and now and then stealing a shy glance from under their eyebrows, until, as if by one impulse, they scampered away and so turned an angle of the gallery; I heard them laughing in triumph at their escape.

The Sketch Book of
Geoffrey Crayon, Gent.,
by Washington Irving, 1820.

In the countries where the disgraceful practice of slavery yet remains, a young slave child would appear to be considered as a desirable present, and advertisements to the following effect may be occasionally seen, outraging the feelings, and showing an utter indifference to the common ties of humanity. 'To be sold, a little child, two years of age, very pretty, and well adapted for a festival present.' It is to be presumed that this 'very pretty' child had a mother. Poor creature! When will this abomination of man selling his fellow-man cease on the earth? We may remember that about the time of Julius Caesar's wife, we have lately mentioned, and long before America was known, white slaves from Britain were imported into Rome, as valuable articles for the sports of the amphitheatres. However, we must leave slavery to the lash of *Uncle Tom's Cabin;* but in describing a festival peculiarly commemorative of peace, good will, and freedom to man, one could not help raising a voice, however feeble, against such an evil.

Sandys,
Christmastide, 1852.

The grievances I have spoken of were thus summed up by the Parliamentary Committee. After referring to the ill-usage and hardships sustained by the climbing boys it is stated: —

'It is in evidence that (1) they are stolen from (and sold by) their parents, and inveigled out of workhouses; (2) that in order to conquer the natural repugnance of the infants to ascend the narrow and dangerous chimneys to clean which their labour is required, blows are used; that pins are forced into their feet by the boy that follows them up the chimney, in order to compel them to ascend it, and that lighted straw has been applied for that purpose; (3) that the children are subject to sores and bruises, and wounds and burns on their thighs, knees, and elbows; and that it will require many months before the extremities of the elbows and knees become sufficiently hard to resist the excoriations to which they are at first subject.'

With regard to the *stealing or kidnapping of children* – for there was often a difficulty in procuring climbing boys – I find mention in the evidence, as of a matter, but not a very frequent matter, of notoriety. One stolen child was sold to a master sweeper for £8 8s.

Mayhew,
London Labour and the London Poor, 1861.

The Book of Directions for the taking those most safe and Famous Medicines Intituled *Pulvis Benedictus,* etc. is now Printed, with an Historical Account of *Worms,*

Collected from the best Authors, as well Ancient as Modern, and Experiments proved by that Admiral Invention of the *Microscope;* also *Diagnostick* Signs of *Worms,* and Signs of Health in Children, with the Various causes of *Vermiculars*: . . . This Book is given with each Paper of Powder, which contains Nine Doses: Price Two Shillings, and ought to be perused by all prudent Parents, that Prize the Wellfare of their Children; Prepared by *R. C. Chymist,* Living at the *Golden-Ball* in *Devon-shire-street,* without *Bishops-gate.*

The London Intelligence, 1688.

BOOKS FOR YOUTH

Printed for Vernor and Hood, No. 31, Poultry.

TALES of the COTTAGE; or Stories Moral and Amusing, for young persons; written on the plan of that celebrated work, The Tales of the Castle. By Madame Genlis. Half bound, vellum back, with elegant Frontispiece, 2s.

The Times, 1798.

Books crowd the world to excess, and our children, like ourselves, suffer from plethora. Naturally omnivorous, they devour all that comes in their way, and as every uncle believes that a picture-book for the younger and a *novelette* for the elder scions is the most appropriate and improving present he can make, they are in general supplied with abundant provision for their undiscriminating appetites. It would be well, however, if we would enforce upon our children some degree of abstemiousness, and put some limit to their literary inquiries. Children naturally love clear images and distinct recollections, and, for the most part, they enjoy them; but it is possible to fill their minds with a confused medley of ideas, the chaotic residuum of all that has passed through their apprehensions; − where Aladdin and the Little Naturalist, Captain Cook and Cinderella, Moral Tales and the Habits of Monkeys, play their shifting parts, and mingle in inextricable entanglement. The enervation of the powers of attention and memory are not the only evils of allowing children constantly to turn to new resources instead of exhausting the old. It is scarcely a less evil that they never thoroughly know, and therefore never thoroughly enjoy, the best things which are set before them.

The Prospective Review, 1855.

The garlic ointment is a well known remedy in North-Britain for the chin-cough. It is made by beating in a mortar garlic with an equal quantity of hogs lard, butter, or oil. With this the soles of the feet may be rubbed twice or thrice a day, or it may be spread thin upon a rag, and applied as a plaster. It should be renewed every night and morning at least, as the garlic soon loses its virtue. This is an exceedingly good medicine both in the chin-cough, and in most other coughs of an obstinate nature. It ought not however to be used when the patient is very hot or feverish, lest it increase these symptoms.

Buchan, *Domestic Medicine*, 1769.

About the year 1618 in France *The True Prophecies or Prognostications of Michael Nostradamus* was used as a Primer for children. Here is a sample of what the children learnt: –

'Out of the deepest part of the west of
  Europe,
From poor people a young child shall be
  born,
Who with his tongue shall seduce many
  people,
His fame shall increase in the Eastern
  Kingdom.'

If any enquire where this Education may be performed; such may be informed, That a *School* is lately erected for Gentlewomen at *Tottenham-high-Cross*, within four miles of *London*, in the Road to *Ware*; where Mistress *Makin* is Governess, who was sometimes Tutoress to the Princess *Elizabeth* Daughter to King Charles the First; Where by the blessing of God, Gentlewomen may be instructed in the Principles of *Religion*; and in all manner of Sober and Vertuous Education:

More particularly, in all things ordinarily taught in other Schools:

As,
Works of all sorts
Dancing
Musick
Singing
Writing
Keeping Accompts
} Half the time to be spent in these Things.

The other half to be imployed in gaining the *Latin* and *French* Tongues; and those that please, may learn *Greek* and *Hebrew*, the *Italian* and *Spanish*: In all which this Gentlewoman hath a competent knowledge.

Gentlewomen of eight or nine years old, that can read well, may be instructed in a year or two (according to their Parts) in the *Latin* and *French* Tongues; by such plain and short Rules, accommodated to the *Grammar* of the *English* Tongue, that they may easily keep what they have learned, and recover what they shall lose; as those that learn Musick by Notes.

Those that will bestow longer time, may learn the other Languages, aforementioned, as they please.

Repositories also for Visibles shall be prepared; by which, from beholding the things, Gentlewomen may learn the Names, Natures, Values, and Use of *Herbs, Shrubs, Trees, Mineral-Juices, Metals* and *Stones.*

Those that please, may learn *Limning, Preserving, Pastry* and *Cookery.*

Those that will allow longer time, may attain some general Knowledge in *Astronomy, Geography;* but especially in *Arithmetick* and *History,* Languages, and learn onely *Experimental Philosophy;* and more, or fewer of the other things aforementioned, as they incline.

The Rate certain shall be 20 *l. per annum;* But if a competent improvement be made in the Tongues, and the other things aforementioned, as shall be agreed upon, then something more will be expected. But the Parents shall judge what shall be deserved by the Undertaker.

Those that think these Things Improbable or Impracticable, may have further account every *Tuesday* at Mr *Masons* Coffee House in *Cornhil,* near the Royal Exchange; and *Thursdays* at the Bolt and Tun in *Fleetstreet,* between the hours of three and six in the Afternoons, by some Person, whom Mris. *Makin* shall appoint.

An Essay to Revive the Antient Education of Gentlewomen, 1673.

ABOUT HENRY VI
born December 1421.

In a very naïvely worded document, the privy council, writing as if the king were giving his directions to his governess himself, requests dame Alice 'from time to time reasonably to chastise us, as the case may require, without being held accountable or molested for the same at any future time. The well-beloved dame Alice (being a very wise and expert person) is to teach us courtesy and *nurture,* (good manners,) and many things convenient for our royal person to learn.'

Strickland,
Lives of the Queens of England, 1875.

This advertisement from *The Times*:
'WANTED immediately, an APPRENTICE to a CHEMIST and DRUGGIST, in an old-established House in the City, where he will have an opportunity of acquiring a thorough knowledge of every branch of the business, and will be treated as one of the family. A genteel Premium is required.

Apply to Messrs. Harris, Son, and Taylor, Druggists, St Paul's Churchyard.'

August, 1798.

Makes us understand the following:
'Blunders of Apothecaries' and Chemists' Boys.

Never, if you are wise, take any thing from the hands of a boy in a drug shop; for death may be the consequence. In the first place, most boys are very ignorant, and cannot well be otherwise; but even where they know a little, they are almost uniformly careless and heedless, and will as readily give you oxalic acid as Epsom salts, and arsenic, as calomel.'

Buchan, *The Cottage Physician,* 1825.

DISTINGUISHED
DECEMBER
BABIES

CHRISTINA ROSSETTI
born December 1830.

TO MY MOTHER

TO-DAY'S your natal day;
    Sweet flowers I bring;
Mother, accept, I pray,
    My offering.

And may you happy live,
    And long us bless;
Receiving, as you give,
    Great happiness.

                    1842.

57

THOMAS CARLYLE
born December 1795.

Speaking of his father . . .

'My memory dawns (or grows light) at the first aspect of the stream; of the pool spanned by a wooden bow without railing, and a single plank broad. He lifted me against his thigh with his right hand, and walked carelessly along till we were over. My face was turned rather downwards. I looked into the deep clear water and its reflected skies with terror, yet with confidence that he could save me . . . He was very kind, and I loved him. All around this is dusk or night before and after.'

Reminiscences, by Thomas Carlyle, 1881.

WARREN HASTINGS
born December 1732.

'To lie beside the margin of that stream, and muse, was,' said Mr Hastings to a friend who was frequently his guest after the termination of his persecutions, 'one of my favourite recreations; and there, one bright summer's day, when I was scarcely seven years old, I well remember that I first formed the determination to purchase back Daylesford. I was then literally dependent upon those whose condition scarcely raised them above the pressure of absolute want; yet somehow or another, the child's dream, as it did not appear unreasonable at the moment, so in after years it never faded away . . . I have lived to accomplish it.'

POPE LEO X
born December 1475.

Giovanni, the second son of Lorenzo, was destined from his infancy to the church. Early brought forward into public view, and strongly impressed with a sense of the necessity of a grave deportment, he seems never to have been a child. At seven years of age he was admitted into holy orders, and received the tonsura from Gentile, bishop of Arezzo. From thenceforth he was called Messer Giovanni, and was soon afterwards declared capable of ecclesiastical preferment.

Roscoe, *The Life of Lorenzo de' Medici*, 1847.

BEETHOVEN
born December 1770.

... I cannot help adverting to a tale, so
ingeniously invented and so frequently repeated,
relative to a spider, which 'whenever little
Ludwig was playing in his closet on the violin,
would let itself down from the ceiling and
alight upon the instrument, and which his
mother, on discovering her son's companion,
one day destroyed, whereupon little Ludwig
dashed his violin to shatters.' This is nothing
more than a tale. *Great* Ludwig, highly as this
fiction amused him, never would admit
that he had the least recollection of such a
circumstance. On the contrary, he declared
that it was much more likely that everything,
even to the very flies and spiders, should have
fled out of the hearing of his horrid scraping.
Moscheles, *The Life of Beethoven*, 1841.

ADMIRAL LORD COCHRANE
born December 1775.

By way of initiation into the mysteries
of the military profession, I was placed

under the tuition of an old sergeant, whose first lessons well accorded with his instructions, not to pay attention to my foibles. My hair, cherished with boyish pride, was formally cut, and plastered back with a vile composition of candle-grease and flour, to which was added the torture incident to the cultivation of an incipient *queue.* My neck, from childhood open to the lowland breeze, was encased in an inflexible leathern collar or stock, selected according to my preceptor's notions of military propriety; these almost verging on strangulation. A blue semi-military tunic, with red collar and cuffs, in imitation of the Windsor uniform, was provided, and to complete the *tout ensemble,* my father, who was a determined Whig partisan, insisted on my wearing yellow waistcoat and breeches; yellow being the Whig colour, of which I was admonished never to be ashamed. A more certain mode of calling into action the dormant obstinacy of a sensitive, high-spirited lad, could not have been devised than that of converting him into a caricature, hateful to himself, and ridiculous to others.

. . . a new windmill was set up near
Grantham, in the way to Gunnerby, which is
now demolished, this country chiefly using
water mills. Our lad's imitating spirit was
soon excited and by frequently prying into
the fabric of it, as they were making it, he
became master enough to make a very perfect
model thereof, and it was said to be as clean
and curious a piece of workmanship, as the
original. This sometimes he would set upon
the housetop, where he lodged, and clothing
it with sail-cloth, the wind would readily
turn it; but what was most extraordinary in
its composition was, that he put a mouse
into it, which he called the miller, and that
the mouse made the mill turn round when
he pleased; and he would joke too upon the
miller eating the corn that was put in. Some
say that he tied a string to the mouse's tail,
which was put into a wheel, like that of
turn-spit dogs, so that pulling the string,
made the mouse go forward by way of
resistance, and this turned the mill. Others

suppose there was some corn placed above the wheel, this the mouse endeavouring to get to, made it turn.

Collections for the History of the Town and Soke of Grantham, by Turner, 1806.

JOSEPH GRIMALDI
born December 1778.

In 1782, he first appeared at Sadler's Wells . . . He played a monkey, and had to accompany the clown (his father) throughout the piece.

In one of the scenes, the clown used to lead him on by a chain attached to his waist, and with this chain he would swing him round and round, at arm's length, with the utmost velocity. One evening, when this feat was in the act of performance, the chain broke, and he was hurled a considerable distance into the pit, fortunately without sustaining the slightest injury; for he was flung by a miracle into the very arms of an old gentleman who was sitting gazing at the stage with intense interest.

Whitehead,
Memoirs of Joseph Grimaldi, 1846.

GAMES
for the
DECEMBER
BABY

WITH the mother's knee as a steed:
Ride, baby, ride,
Pretty baby shall ride,
And have little puppy-dog tied to her side,
And little pussy-cat tied to the other,
And away she shall ride to see her grandmother;
To see her grandmother,
To see her grandmother in London town.

Nursery Rhymes, Tales and Jingles,
London, 1844.

HODDY-DODDY. — 'Hoddy-Doddy, all legs and no body,' affords a source of amusement and wonder to children of all ages at Christmas time or on birthdays, for it should not be often exhibited, and then only at night, for obvious reasons. 'Hoddy-Doddy' is the figure of a man cut out in thin paper two or three inches long, with thin long legs and arms, and very little body. One end of a long hair is secured to him by a minute piece of white wax, and the other end to a polished round table. The hair must be less in length than half the diameter of the table. When all is ready, the children come into the room and are collected round the table, with their hands tied behind them, and are told to blow. Hoddy-Doddy begins to leap and jump from side to side of the table. The harder they blow, the more he leaps, but no blowing will make him leap off. At last mamma puts her hand on the table (to remove the wax), and the next time they blow, off he jumps, as merrily as possible, amid shouts of laughter, and does not make his appearance till the next birthday in winter.

Kingston, *Infant Amusements*, 1867.

In acting charades, and above all in tableaux, coloured light is often a great improvement; indeed, sometimes it is indispensable . . .

Mix some common salt with spirits of wine in a metal cup, and set it upon a wire frame over a spirit lamp. When the cup becomes heated, the other lights on the stage should be extinguished, and that of the spirit lamp shaded in some way. The result will be that the whole group, faces, dresses, &c., will be of a strong yellow tint. This is used if you act Spenser's 'Cave of Mammon' or 'Plutus'.

As green fire is not of much use, and it is made with a portion of arsenic in it, we do not give directions for it.

The Home Book of Pleasure and Instruction,
by Laura Jewry, 1867.

A
DECEMBER
CHILD IN
FICTION

HE went along a passage and reached the staircase; here he heard a very gentle sound, like the breathing of a child. He followed this sound, and reached a triangular closet under the stairs, or, to speak more correctly, formed by the stairs themselves. Here, among old hampers and potsherds, in dust and cobwebs, there was a bed, if we may apply the term to a paillasse so rotten as to show the straw, and a blanket so torn as to show the mattress. There were no sheets, and all this lay on the ground; in this bed Cosette was sleeping. The man walked up and gazed at her; Cosette was fast asleep and full dressed; in winter she did not take off her clothes, that she might be a little warmer. She was holding to her bosom the doll, whose large open eyes glistened in the darkness; from time to time she gave a heavy sigh, as if about to awake, and pressed the doll almost convulsively in her arms. There was nothing by her bedside but one of her wooden shoes. Through an open door close by a large dark room could be seen, through which the stranger entered. At the end, two little white beds were visible through a glass door, and which belonged to Eponine and Azelma. Behind this a wicker curtainless cradle was half hidden, in which slept the little boy who had been crying all the evening.

The stranger conjectured that this room communicated with that of the Thenárdiers. He was about to return, when his eye fell on the chimney, one of those vast inn chimneys, in which there is always so little fire when there is a frost, and which are so cold to look at. In this chimney there was no fire, not even ashes; but what there was in it attracted the traveller's attention. He saw two little child's shoes of coquettish shape and unequal size; and the traveller recollected the graceful and immemorial custom of children who place their shoe in the chimney on Christmas night, in order to obtain some glittering present from their good fairy in the darkness. Eponine and Azelma had not failed in this observance. The traveller bent down; the fairy, that is, the mother, had already paid her visit, and in each shoe a handsome ten-sous piece could be seen shining. The man rose and was going away, when he observed another object in the darkest corner of the hearth; he looked at it, and recognized a hideous wooden shoe, half broken and covered with ashes and dried mud. It was Cosette's; with the touching confidence of children who may be disappointed, but are never discouraged, she had also placed her shoe in the chimney. Hope in a child that has never known aught but despair, is a sublime and affecting thing. There was nothing in this shoe; but the stranger felt in his pocket and laid a louis d'or in it; then he crept noiselessly back to his bedroom.

Victor Hugo, *Les Misérables,*
Authorized English Translation, 1862.

LETTERS
FROM TWO
ROYAL DECEMBER
CHILDREN

A LETTER written at the age of eight by Elizabeth, daughter of Charles I:

My Lords,

I account myself very miserable that I must have my servants taken from me, and strangers put to me. You promised me that you would have a care of me, and I hope you will show it in preventing so great a grief, as this would be to me. I pray, my lords, consider of it, and give me cause to thank you, and to rest
your loving Friend,
Elizabeth.
To the right honourable the lords and peers in Parliament.

Excerpt from a letter written to Queen Mary by Henry Stuart, Lord Darnley at the age of nine (born December, 1545):

. . . I am inflamed and stirred even now, my tender age notwithstanding, to be serving your Grace, wishing every hair in my head to be a worthy soldier of that same self heart, mind, and stomach, that I am of. But whereas I perceive that neither my wit, power, nor years are at this present corresponding to this my good will, these shall be, therefore (most gracious Princess), most humbly rendering unto your Majesty immortal thanks for your rich chain, and other your Highness' sundry gifts given to me, without any my deservings, from time to time. Trusting in God, one day of my as bounden duty to endeavour myself with my faithful hearty service to remember the same.

RHYMES
for the
DECEMBER
BABY

C OLD December brings the sleet,
Blazing fire and Christmas
    treat.
    Sara Coleridge (1802–1852).

Down the chimney St Nicholas came with a
    bound.
He was dressed all in fur, from his head to his
    foot,

And his clothes were all tarnished with ashes
    and soot;
A bundle of Toys he had flung on his back,
And he looked like a pedlar just opening his
    pack.
His eyes – how they twinkled! his dimples,
    how merry!
His cheeks were like roses, his nose like a
    cherry!
His droll little mouth was drawn up like
    a bow,
And the beard of his chin was as white as
    the snow;
The stump of a pipe he held tight in his
    teeth,
And the smoke it encircled his head like a
    wreath;
He had a broad face and a little round belly,
That shook when he laughed, like a bowl-full
    of jelly.
He was chubby and plump, a right jolly old elf,
And I laughed when I saw him, in spite of
    myself,
A wink of his eye and a twist of his head,
Soon gave me to know I had nothing to
    dread;

He spoke not a word, but went straight to
    his work,
And fill'd all the stockings; then turned with
    a jerk,
And laying his finger aside of his nose,
And giving a nod, up the chimney he rose;
He sprang to his sleigh, to his team gave a
    whistle,
And away they all flew like the down of a
    thistle.
But I heard him exclaim, ere he drove out of
    sight,
'Happy Christmas to all, and to all a good
    night.'

             Clement C. Moore (1779–1863).

A Child this day is born,
  A Child of high renown,
Most worthy of a sceptre,
  A sceptre and a crown.
    Novels, Novels, Novels,
      Novels, sing all we may,

Because the King of all Kings
Was born this blessed day.
Christmas Carols,
collected by Sandys, 1833.

THE VIRGIN'S CRADLE-HYMN

Dormi, Jesu! Mater ridet
Quae tam dulcem somnum videt,
  Dormi Jesu! blandule!
Si non dormis, Mater plorat,
Inter fila cantans orat,
  Blande, veni, somnule.

ENGLISH

Sleep, sweet babe! my cares beguiling:
Mother sits beside thee smiling;

Sleep, my darling, tenderly!
If thou sleep not, mother mourneth,
Singing as her wheel she turneth:
Come, soft slumber, balmily!

A PRAYER

Forgive me, Lord, for thy dear Son,
The ills that I this day have done;
That with the world, myself, and Thee,
I, ere I sleep, at peace may be.

Bishop Thomas Ken (1637–1711).

GOODNIGHT
to the
DECEMBER
BABY

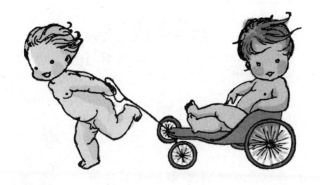

BIRTHDAY keeping apart, the Christmas month is a wonderful one in which to be born. December is the children's month, all over the world, and is always connected with presents. It is, too, full of legends, including the popular one that children born on Christmas Eve throughout their lives can hear, on that day, the animals talk at midnight. I have often tried this out, and never an animal has spoken in front of me.

If you could choose gifts for your December baby what would you, apart from health, wealth, and happiness, select? It is an age-old problem, for gifts for her child which might seem desirable to the mother could so well be unsuited to the adult the baby grows up to be. It is easy to imagine a girl craving for an academic career, who thanks to her mother's wish, finds herself a film star. Or the man who thanks to a wish, becomes a great political figure, but is at heart a country parson.

It is pleasant as you drop off to sleep to think of wishes, but would you make a wish for your baby if you could? Or would you have it just the way it is? Goodnight.

Noel Streatfeild